First book of Numbers

Written by Peter Patilla
Illustrated by David Melling

OXFORD

UNIVERSITY PRESS

For my grandchildren – P.P.
For Štefica, Žarko, Petra, Filip, Daraja Filipović – D.M.

OXFORD
UNIVERSITY PRESS

Great Clarendon Street, Oxford OX2 6DP

Oxford University Press is a department of the University of Oxford.
It furthers the University's objective of excellence in research, scholarship,
and education by publishing worldwide in

Oxford   New York

Auckland Cape Town Dar es Salaam Hong Kong Karachi
Kuala Lumpur Madrid Melbourne Mexico City Nairobi
New Delhi Shanghai Taipei Toronto

With offices in

Argentina Austria Brazil Chile Czech Republic France Greece
Guatemala Hungary Italy Japan Poland Portugal Singapore
South Korea Switzerland Thailand Turkey Ukraine Vietnam

Oxford is a registered trade mark of Oxford University Press
in the UK and in certain other countries

Text copyright © Peter Patilla 2000
Illustration copyright © David Melling 2000

British Library Cataloguing in Publication Data

Data available

ISBN-13: 978-0-19-911215-9
ISBN-10: 0-19-911215-0

1 3 5 7 9 10 8 6 4 2

Printed in Singapore

Contents

Packing

Numbers

0   zero   nothing

1   one   1

2   two   2

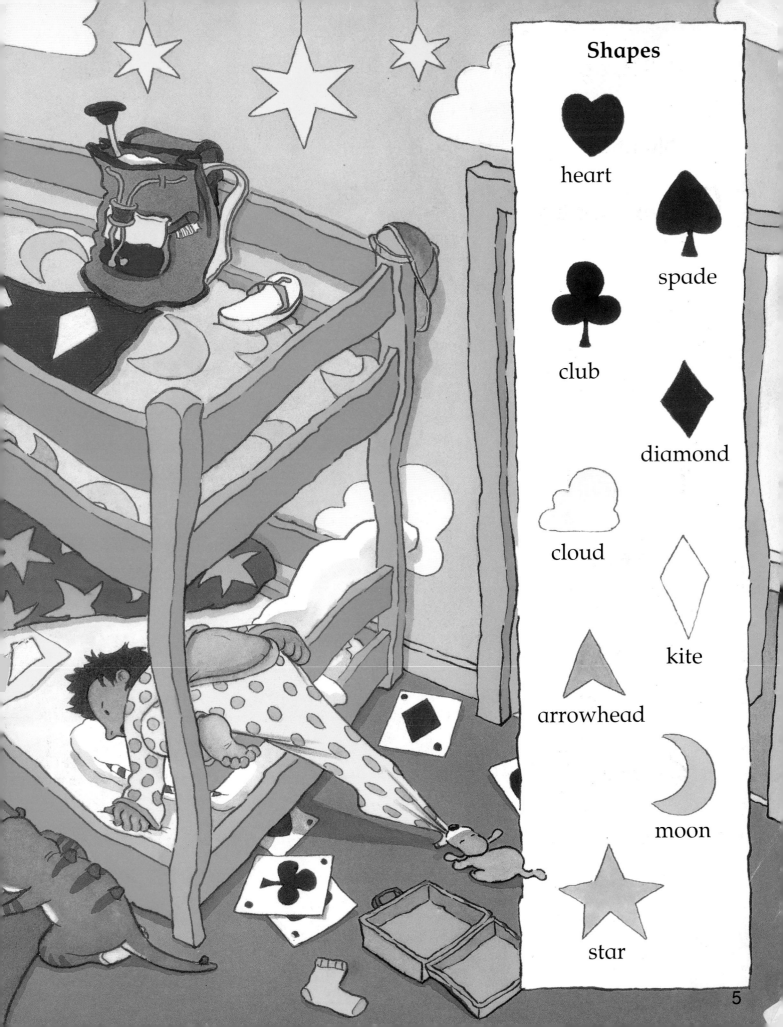

Shapes

heart

spade

club

diamond

cloud

kite

arrowhead

moon

star

5

Countdown

Numbers

3 three **3**

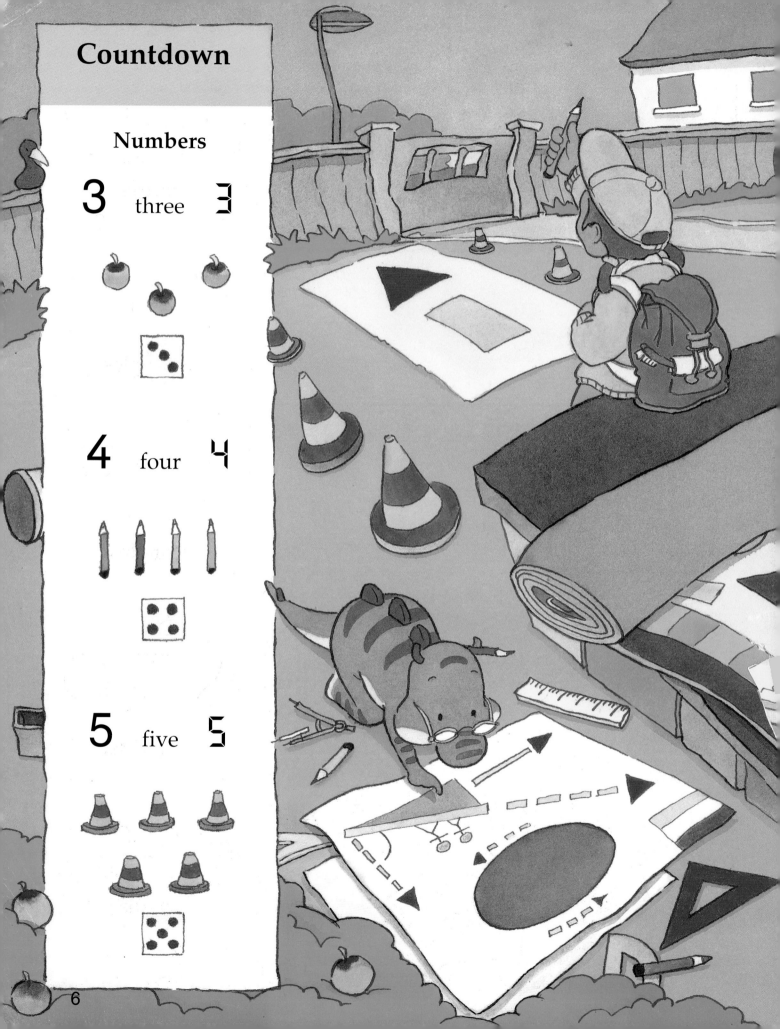

4 four **4**

5 five **5**

6

Shapes

squares

rectangles

triangles

circles

ovals

Numbers

6 6
six

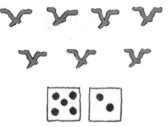

7 7
seven

8 8
eight

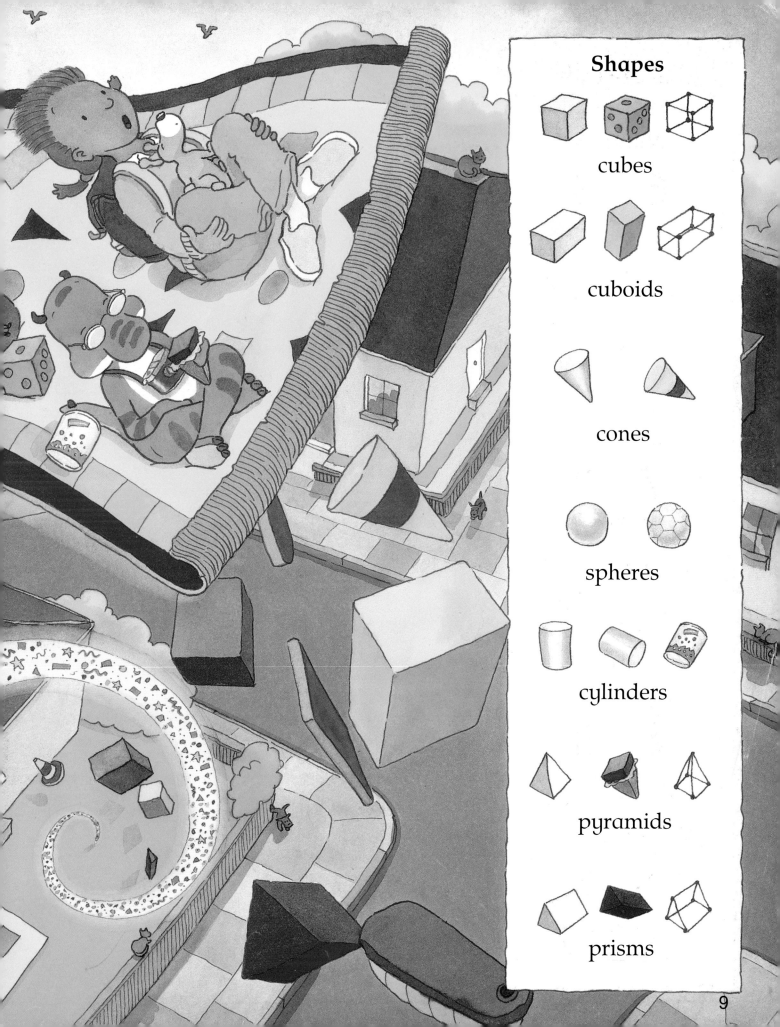

Shapes

cubes

cuboids

cones

spheres

cylinders

pyramids

prisms

Flying High

Numbers

9 9
nine

10 10
ten

11 11
eleven

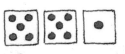

Colours

red

green

yellow

blue

orange

brown

pink

purple

grey

white

black

11

Feeding Fish

Numbers

12 12
twelve

13 13
thirteen

14 14
fourteen

Patterns

spirals

loops

wavy lines

zig-zags

square teeth

peaks

13

Numbers

15

fifteen

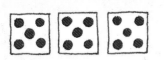

16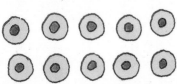

sixteen

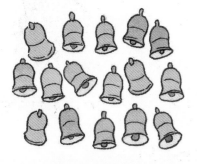

Patterns

rings

stripes

spotted

plaid

chequered

criss-cross

overlapping

paw prints

tessellated

repeating patterns

Penguin Fun

Numbers

17

seventeen

18

eighteen

16

Weight and Capacity

heavy

light

lighter

heavier

heavy

very heavy

full

half full

empty

full

nearly full

very full

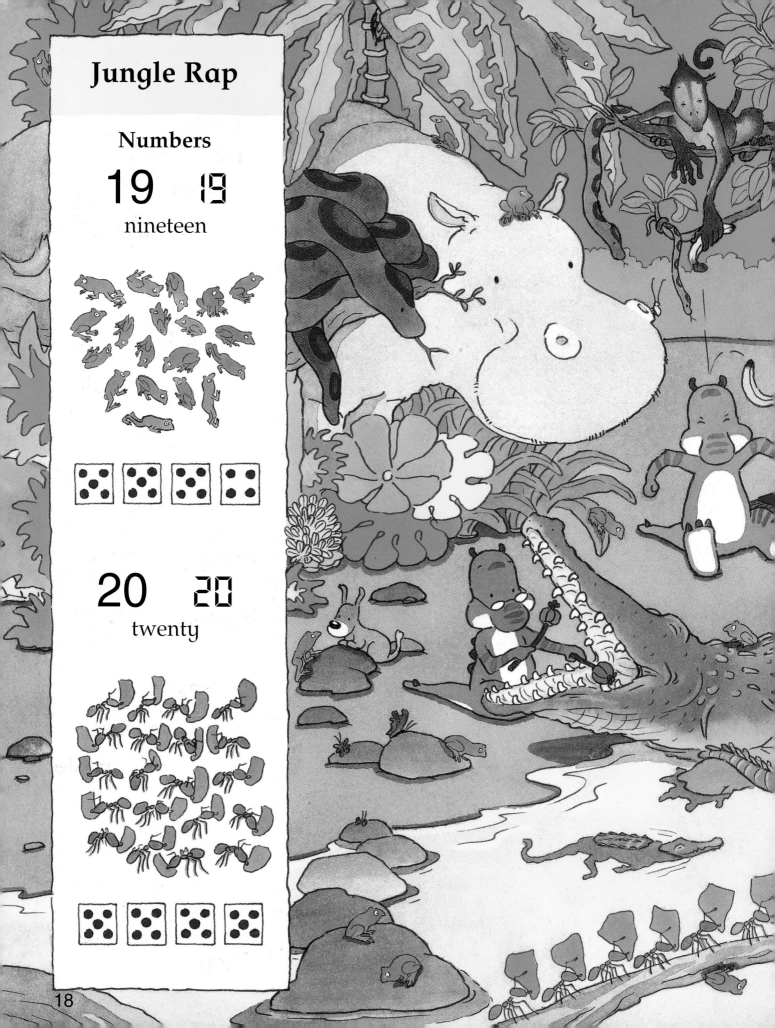

Jungle Rap

Numbers

19 19
nineteen

20 20
twenty

Size words

fat

thin

very thin

large

small

very small

big

bigger

biggest

small

smaller

smallest

huge

tiny

19

Cake Break

Fractions

$\frac{1}{2}$  half

$\frac{1}{4}$ quarter

$\frac{1}{3}$ third

$\frac{3}{4}$ three quarters

whole

nearly a whole

a small part

Length

long   short

thick   thin

deep   shallow

tall   short

high   low

21

Landing

Even Numbers

2 ⭐⭐

4 ⭐⭐ ⭐⭐

6 ⭐⭐⭐ ⭐⭐⭐

8 ⭐⭐⭐⭐ ⭐⭐⭐⭐

10 ⭐⭐⭐⭐⭐ ⭐⭐⭐⭐⭐

Odd Numbers

1 •

3

5

7

9

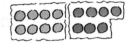

Length

long

longer

longest

tall

taller

tallest

short

shorter

shortest

23

Home to Sleep

Order

1st 2nd 3rd

3rd 2nd 1st

first last

1st
2nd
3rd
4th
5th
6th
7th
8th
9th
10th

Position

above
top
bottom
below

left right
between

in
out

behind
in front

top
middle
bottom

Days of the Week

Monday

Tuesday

Wednesday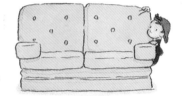

Thursday

Friday

Saturday

Sunday

Months of the Year

January

February

March

April

May

June

July

August

September

October

November

December

Seasons

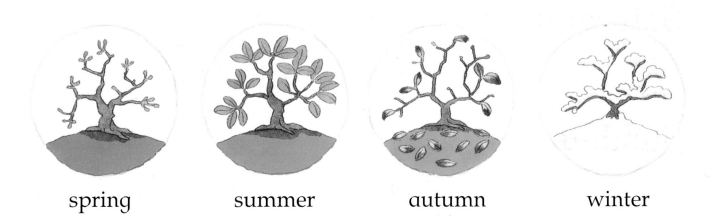

spring

summer

autumn

winter

Numbers 0 – 100

0	zero
1	one
2	two
3	three
4	four
5	five
6	six
7	seven
8	eight
9	nine
10	ten
11	eleven
12	twelve
13	thirteen
14	fourteen
15	fifteen
16	sixteen
17	seventeen
18	eighteen
19	nineteen
20	twenty

10 ten	
20 twenty	
30 thirty	
40 forty	
50 fifty	
60 sixty	
70 seventy	
80 eighty	
90 ninety	
100 one hundred	

Index

part, small	20	shorter	23	thirteen	12,28
patterns	13,15	shortest	23	thirty	29
paw prints	15	six	8,22,28	three	6,22,28
peaks	13	sixteen	14,28	three quarters	20
pink	11	sixty	29	Thursday	26
plaid	15	size	19	tiny	19
position	25	small	19	top	25
prisms	9	smaller	19	triangles	7
purple	11	smallest	19	Tuesday	26
pyramids	9	spade	5	twelve	12,28
		spheres	9	twenty	18,28,29
		spirals	13	two	4,22,28
quarter	20	spotted	15		
		spring	27		
rectangles	7	square teeth	13	wavy lines	13
red	11	squares	7	Wednesday	26
repeating patterns	15	star	5	week	26
right	25	stripes	15	weight	17
rings	15	summer	27	white	11
		Sunday	26	whole	20
				winter	27
Saturday	26				
seasons	27	tall	21,23		
September	27	taller	23	year	27
seven	8,22,28	tallest	23	yellow	11
seventeen	16,28	ten	10,22,28,29		
seventy	29	tessellated	15		
shallow	21	thick	21	zero	4,28
shapes	5,7,9	thin	19,21	zig-zags	13
short	21,23	third	20